Lulu Saves the Day!

Supersmart Pig

BY SARAH EASON
ILLUSTRATED BY DIEGO VAISBERG

BEARPORT
PUBLISHING

Minneapolis, Minnesota

Credits: 20, © Nupook538/Shutterstock; 21, © AdaCo/Shutterstock; 22, © Budimir Jevtic/Shutterstock; 23, © Galitsin/Shutterstock.

Bearport Publishing Company Product Development Team
President: Jen Jenson; Director of Product Development: Spencer Brinker;
Senior Editor: Allison Juda; Editor: Charly Haley; Associate Editor: Naomi Reich;
Senior Designer: Colin O'Dea; Associate Designer: Elena Klinkner; Associate
Designer: Kayla Eggert; Product Development Assistant: Anita Stasson

Produced by Calcium
Editor: Jennifer Sanderson; Proofreader: Harriet McGregor; Designer: Paul
Myerscough; Picture Researcher: Rachel Blount

DISCLAIMER: This graphic story is a dramatization based on true events. It is intended to give the reader a sense of the narrative rather than a presentation of actual details as they occurred.

Library of Congress Cataloging-in-Publication Data

Names: Eason, Sarah, author. | Vaisberg, Diego, illustrator.
Title: Lulu saves the day! : supersmart pig / by Sarah Eason ; illustrated
by Diego Vaisberg.
Other titles: Supersmart pig
Description: Minneapolis, Minnesota : Bearport Publishing Company, [2023] |
Series: Animal masterminds | Includes bibliographical references and
index.
Identifiers: LCCN 2022038735 (print) | LCCN 2022038736 (ebook) | ISBN
9798885094320 (hardcover) | ISBN 9798885095549 (paperback) | ISBN
9798885096690 (ebook)
Subjects: LCSH: Potbellied pig--Anecdotes--Juvenile literature. |
Potbellied pig--Anecdotes--Comic books, strips, etc.
Classification: LCC SF393.P74 E27 2023 (print) | LCC SF393.P74 (ebook) |
DDC 636.4/85--dc23/eng/20220829
LC record available at https://lccn.loc.gov/2022038735
LC ebook record available at https://lccn.loc.gov/2022038736

For more information, write to Bearport Publishing, 5357 Penn Avenue South, Minneapolis, MN 55419.

Contents

CHAPTER 1

A Big Pig!

Jack and JoAnn Altsman of Beaver Falls, Pennsylvania, had an unusual pet... a potbellied pig named Lulu. From the time she was a baby, Lulu was a part of their family.

BOY, LULU HAS SURE GROWN FAST!

YES! SHE WENT FROM ONLY A FEW POUNDS TO MORE THAN 200 POUNDS!*

*90 kg

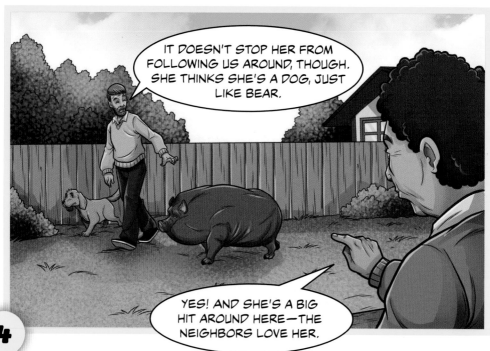

IT DOESN'T STOP HER FROM FOLLOWING US AROUND, THOUGH. SHE THINKS SHE'S A DOG, JUST LIKE BEAR.

YES! AND SHE'S A BIG HIT AROUND HERE—THE NEIGHBORS LOVE HER.

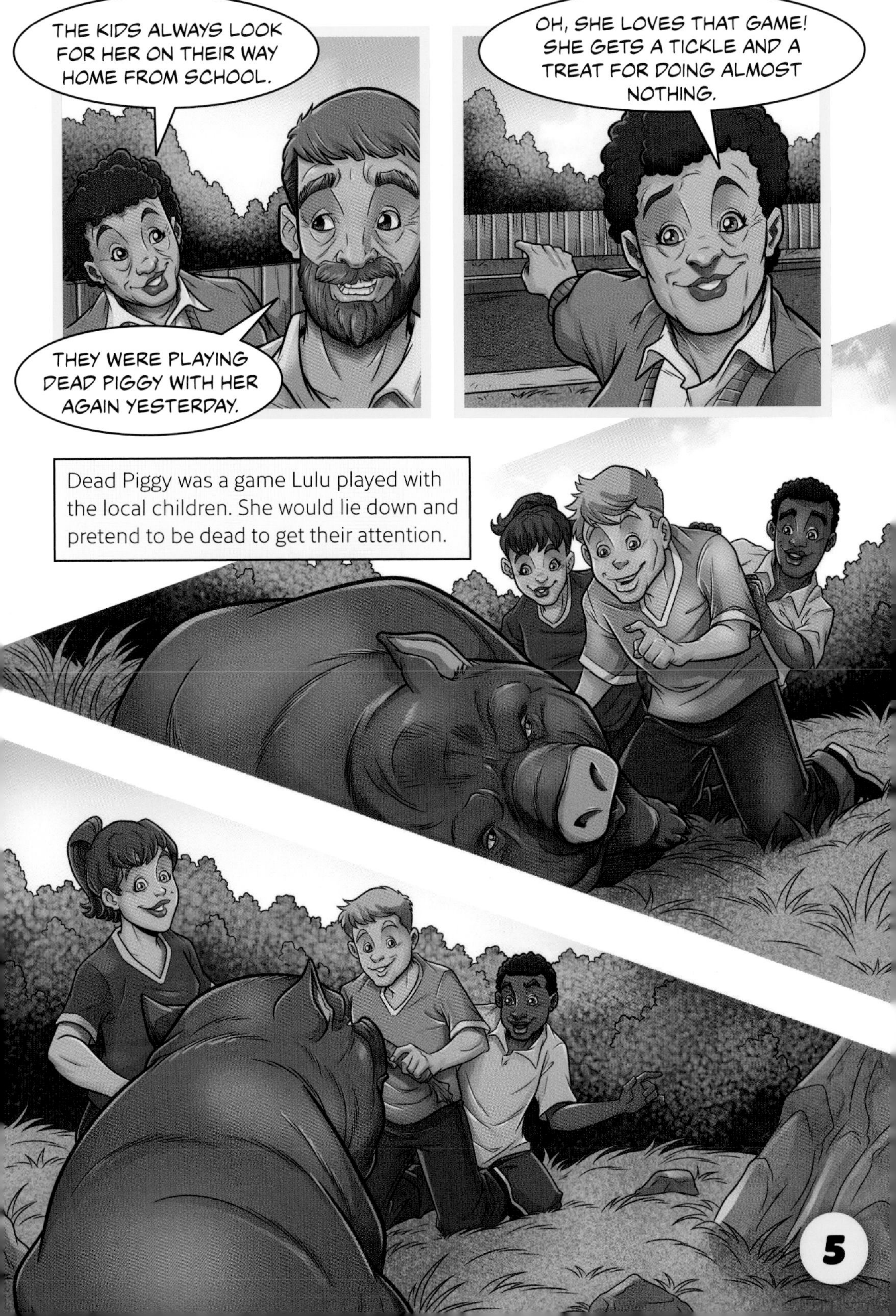
THE KIDS ALWAYS LOOK FOR HER ON THEIR WAY HOME FROM SCHOOL.
THEY WERE PLAYING DEAD PIGGY WITH HER AGAIN YESTERDAY.
OH, SHE LOVES THAT GAME! SHE GETS A TICKLE AND A TREAT FOR DOING ALMOST NOTHING.
Dead Piggy was a game Lulu played with the local children. She would lie down and pretend to be dead to get their attention.

Jack and JoAnn took their pets with them everywhere they went—even on vacation to their trailer near Lake Erie.

One hot summer morning...

OK, JOANN, I'M GOING FISHING.

HAVE FUN!

JoAnn settled in for a relaxing day. But a little later she started to feel unwell.

OUCH! MY CHEST HURTS.

Then, she **collapsed** in the kitchen.

HELP! MY CHEST—IT HURTS.

Bear barked to try and raise the alarm, but nobody heard the dog.

JoAnn did not have a telephone and needed another way to get help.

I'LL TRY TO SMASH A WINDOW.

Still, help didn't come.

JoAnn was having a **heart attack**. Her life was in danger.

HELP! ANYONE... HELP!

Eventually, she lost **consciousness**.

9

CHAPTER 2

Playing Dead

A little while later, JoAnn woke up to Lulu sniffing and grunting near her head.

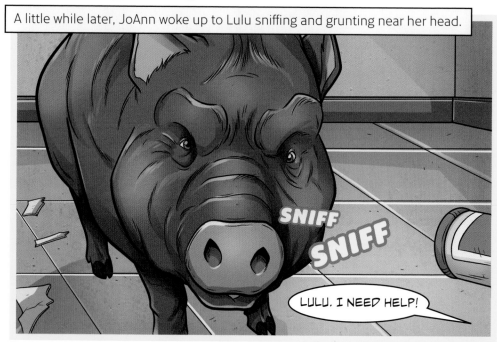

The potbellied pig **shuffled** away and JoAnn began to cry.

JoAnn didn't know it then, but Lulu was on a mission! She tried to squeeze through Bear's dog door. Unfortunately, it wasn't made for a large pig.

Lulu pushed and pushed...

...and made her way outside.

Then, she walked over to the road. She had a plan!

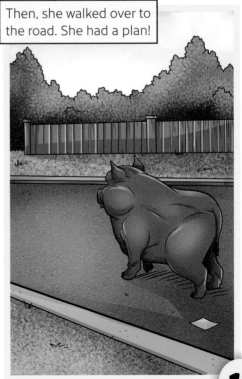

Lulu flopped down on the road and stayed completely still.

LOOK AT THAT! IS THAT HUGE PIG SLEEPING IN THE MIDDLE OF THE ROAD?

WHAT A STRANGE PLACE TO TAKE A NAP!

The car drove away. Lulu's plan to get their attention by playing Dead Piggy didn't work. But she kept trying!

After a while, Lulu went back to check on JoAnn.

SQUEAL!

JoAnn was surprised that Lulu came back.

Lulu sniffed JoAnn and grunted.

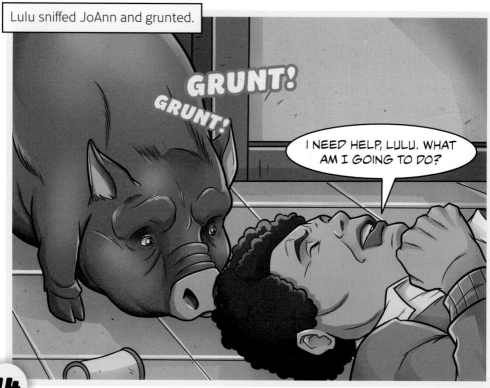

JoAnn lost consciousness once more.

Lulu squeezed back out through the dog door. This time, the frame scratched her skin, and she began to bleed.

Even though she was hurt, Lulu headed back to the road in another attempt to get help.

CHAPTER 3

Saved by Lulu

Finally, a man driving by saw Lulu and stopped.

A PIG! AND THE POOR THING LOOKS INJURED, TOO.

When the stranger got close, Lulu hopped up and rushed back to the trailer.

WAIT! WHERE ARE YOU GOING?

The man followed Lulu and knocked on the door.

HELLO? YOUR PIG IS BLEEDING! IS ANYBODY HOME?

YES! BUT I NEED HELP, TOO... PLEASE CALL 911!

Soon, the **paramedics** arrived to help JoAnn.

Lulu wanted to go with JoAnn in the ambulance.

PLEASE, CAN YOU HELP LULU? THERE'S A FIRST AID KIT UNDER THE SINK.

SORRY, PIGGY. YOU CAN'T COME WITH US.

I'LL TAKE CARE OF HER. I'LL WAIT WITH LULU UNTIL YOUR HUSBAND COMES HOME.

JoAnn was rushed to the hospital for **surgery**.

IF LULU HADN'T GOTTEN HELP, YOU WOULDN'T HAVE MADE IT MUCH LONGER. THAT SUPERSMART PIG SAVED YOUR LIFE!

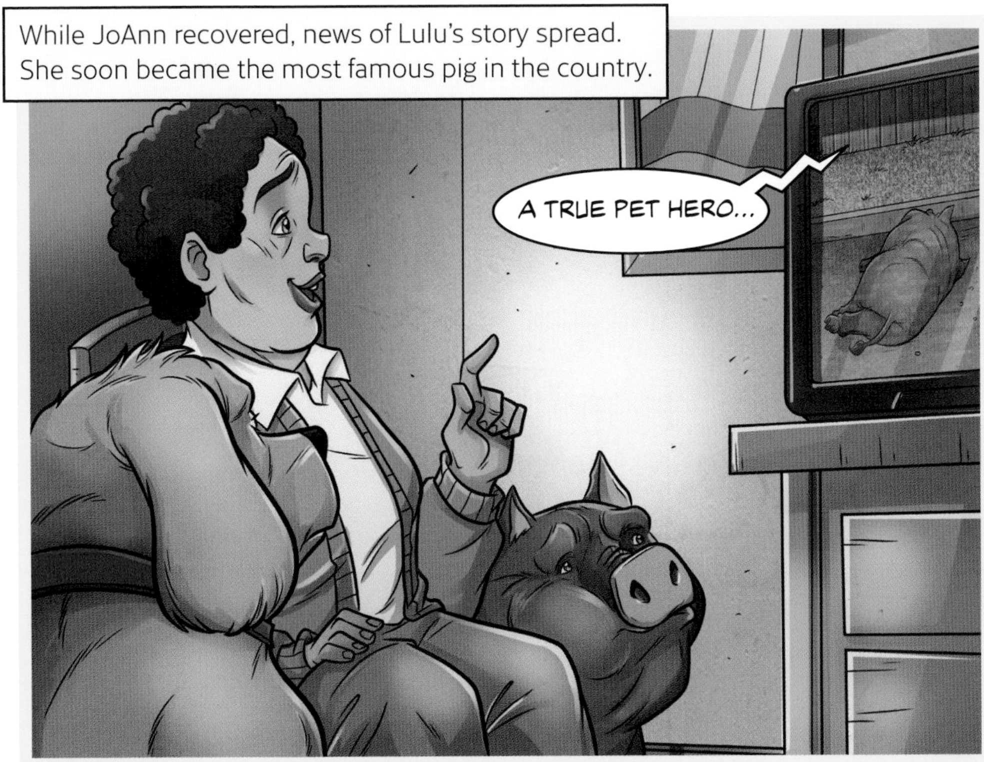
While JoAnn recovered, news of Lulu's story spread. She soon became the most famous pig in the country.
A TRUE PET HERO...

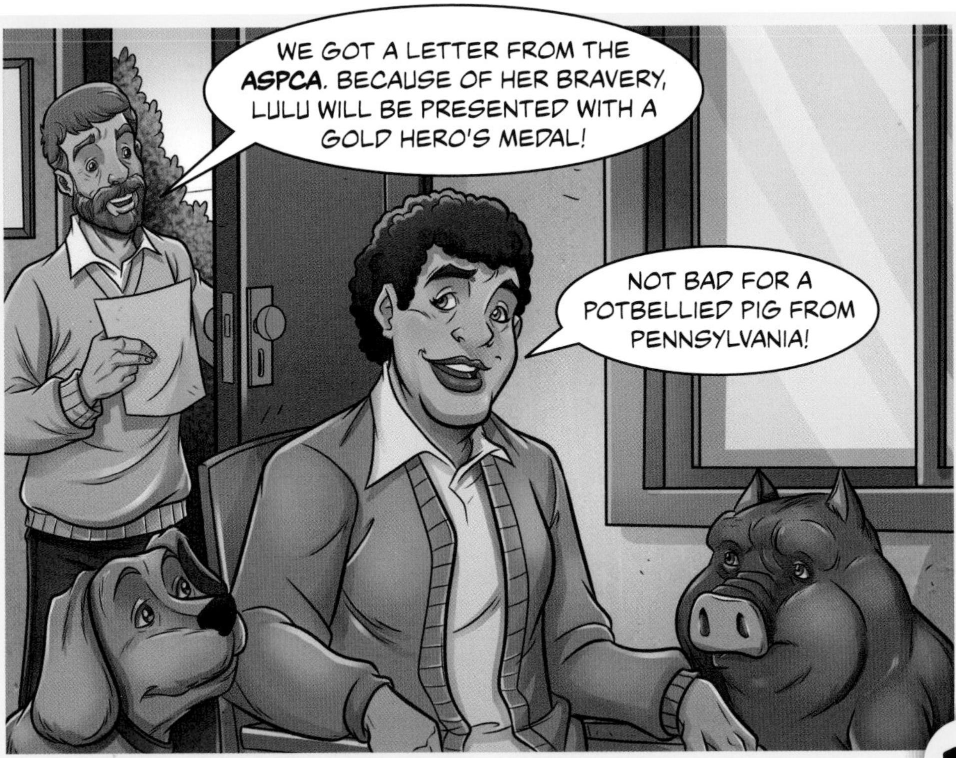
WE GOT A LETTER FROM THE ASPCA. BECAUSE OF HER BRAVERY, LULU WILL BE PRESENTED WITH A GOLD HERO'S MEDAL!
NOT BAD FOR A POTBELLIED PIG FROM PENNSYLVANIA!

All about Potbellied Pigs

Some people keep potbellied pigs as pets. Similar to dogs or cats, these pigs can easily adapt to new places. Let's learn more about these supersmart animals!

- Potbellied pigs can live for up to 20 years.

- The pigs **communicate** by grunting, barking, and squealing.

- Potbellied pigs follow their noses! With their great sense of smell, these pigs can sniff out things that are up to 25 feet (7.6 m) underground.

A MOTHER PIG CAN HAVE A LITTER WITH UP TO 12 PIGLETS.

A FULLY GROWN PIG CAN BE UP TO 25 INCHES (65 CM) LONG AND WEIGH MORE THAN 200 LB (90 KG).

- Naturally curious, potbellied pigs are great diggers! They have been known to dig almost anywhere for something to eat.

- Some scientists believe pigs are the fifth-most **intelligent** animal on Earth.

- Potbellied pigs can become very attached to their owners.

More Smart Pigs

In Germany, a supersmart pig named Moritz amazed his owner by completing a jigsaw puzzle. Moritz was trained to pick up puzzle pieces in his mouth and put them in place. Little by little, the pig put the correct pieces in place to complete the puzzle. Every time Moritz filled in a piece of the puzzle, his owner rewarded him with his favorite snack—popcorn!

Animal behaviorist Dr. Candace Croney once taught a group of pigs to play video games. In the **experiment**, the pigs moved **joysticks** with their mouths or **snouts**. Using the joysticks, the pigs moved an object around to hit targets that appeared on the screen. The pigs were often rewarded with food when they won the video games.

PEOPLE WHO STUDY PIGS SAY THE ANIMALS CAN LEARN TO CARRY OUT NEW TASKS QUICKLY.

Glossary

ASPCA short for the American Society for the Prevention of Cruelty to Animals, an organization that helps various kinds of animals

collapsed fell to the ground

communicate to share information, ideas, feelings and thoughts

consciousness the state of being awake and able to think

experiment a scientific test set up to find the answer to a question

heart attack a sudden problem where a person's heart isn't pumping blood properly

intelligent smart

joysticks devices used to control movements in a video game

paramedics people who are trained to respond to emergencies and take care of injured people until they arrive at the hospital

shuffled walked slowly while dragging the feet on the ground

snouts the long, front part of an animal's head that sticks out; a snout includes the nose and the mouth

surgery treatment for injury or illness performed by cutting into the body

Index

Read More

Buckley, James. *Water Everywhere: Pig Rescue! (Rescued! Animal Escapes)*. Minneapolis: Bearport Publishing Company, 2021.

Mattern, Joanne. *Smartest Animals (Earth's Amazing Animals: Animal Top 10)*. Egremont, MA: Red Chair Press, 2020.

Quinn, Arnold M. *Pigs (Grow with Me)*. Mankato, MN: Creative Education, 2020.

Learn More Online

1. Go to **www.factsurfer.com** or scan the QR code below.
2. Enter "**Lulu Saves the Day**" into the search box.
3. Click on the cover of this book to see a list of websites.